Swedish History

500 Interesting Facts About Sweden

Welcome Aboard, Check Out This Limited-Time Free Bonus!

Ahoy, reader! Welcome to the Ahoy Publications family, and thanks for snagging a copy of this book! Since you've chosen to join us on this journey, we'd like to offer you something special.

Check out the link below for a FREE e-book filled with delightful facts about American History.

But that's not all - you'll also have access to our exclusive email list with even more free e-books and insider knowledge. Well, what are ye waiting for? Click the link below to join and set sail toward exciting adventures in American History.

Access your bonus here: <u>https://ahoypublications.com/</u>

Or, Scan the QR code!

Table of Contents

Introduction

Sweden has a rich and varied history, full of moments that shaped its present state. **From the distant past, when it was a prehistoric society, to its emergence as one of Europe's greatest powers** in the 17th century, this book will explore Sweden's remarkable history.

Beginning with prehistoric Sweden, we'll examine how hunter-gatherers adapted and changed over thousands of years before encountering outsiders from other regions. **As Scandinavia opened to external influences during the Swedish Viking Age,** new opportunities arose for settlement and exploration into unknown lands, leading to increased trade within Europe and beyond. Moving on to **medieval Sweden, we will observe how Christianity took hold in the nation** and how feudalism began to shape society alongside more established customs such as the Law of Jante.

The Kalmar Union saw Denmark take control over much of modern-day Finland, Estonia, Iceland, and Sweden. This period of Danish rule saw religious strife between **the Catholic Church in Denmark and the Lutherans in Sweden**. We will explore how a strong sense of Swedish nationalism emerged during the Swedish Empire.

This book charts the major periods of Swedish history up to the present day, such as **Gustav III's coup d'état, the union with Norway,** and the economic crisis of the 1980s. We will explore **same-sex marriage legislation,** sustainable development policies, and other progressive measures. By exploring each event from different perspectives, **this book aims to provide an informative overall picture of Sweden's complex history.**

Prehistoric Sweden
(c. 12,000 BCE–c. 800 CE)

This chapter will explore **the remarkable history of prehistoric Sweden.** Discover items that have been discovered from ancient sites, and **uncover the different cultures who called Sweden home.** These intriguing insights will give you a better understanding of life during this period.

1. **Prehistoric Sweden dates back to around** 12,000 BCE **(the Paleolithic Age)** when the region was settled by hunter-gatherers from different areas of Europe. **They followed fish and game** throughout the area.

2. **In the Mesolithic period** (c. 8000–4000 BCE), the warming climate melted much of **the glacial ice covering much of Scandinavia,** including Sweden. During this period, the forests began to grow. The people of Sweden began to practice agriculture and animal husbandry.

3. **The Neolithic Age was the last "Stone Age" and lasted from around 4000 to 2300 BCE.** It was a time of great change. People began to build permanent settlements, and they developed new technologies, such as pottery and basic metalworking.

4. **A notable archaeological site is Helgö,** which shows us how prehistoric Swedes lived around 200 CE. Evidence of bronze smithing was found there.

5. **In prehistoric times, many different tribes inhabited Sweden,** including **the Svear** (Swedes), **the Götar** (Goths), and a small number of **Finns.** Though these people were the forebearers of today's Swedes and Finns, it's important to remember their languages and cultures were ever-evolving.

6. **Early Swedish tribes didn't speak a language today's Swedes or Finns would understand.**

7. By 500 BCE, **the Iron Age had started.** Farming was becoming more common, and iron tools improved the output of crops like rye and barley.

8. **As early as 200 CE, trade between Scandinavia and Rome flourished** through intense trading routes via river systems.

9. For many years, **Swedes believed that the first Swedish kings were of the "Yngling"** dynasty and descended from the gods.

10. **Yngvi-Freyr is likely a legendary figure associated with fertility and agriculture.** His reign, if it can be called that, is typically placed in a prehistoric and mythological context, making it difficult to assign specific dates.

11. tIn reality, **Sweden was not united under one king until the early 1500s.**

12. **Prehistoric Swedes wore animal skins for clothing,** which they sewed together with bone needles. They also made jewelry from petrified wood, amber, bronze, silver, and gold.

13. Before Christianity arrived (around 800 CE) and even for a few centuries after, ancient **Scandinavians worshiped gods like Odin, Thor, Freyr, and Freyja.** These gods are still popular today in shows and books about Vikings.

14. **Around 500 CE, simple runic writing became widely used,** which allowed people to mark out territory, label maps, and engrave memorials.

15. In the 600s and 700s CE, **people built fortifications around their villages to protect them from raids by other tribes or neighboring countries.** These fortifications often included earthen walls, ditches, and wooden palisades.

16. **During the late Iron Age,** a few of these fortified villages grew into important towns, such as **Birka** (750 CE), located on **an island in Lake Mälaren.**

17. **Birka became Sweden's first real city.** It eventually developed into a large trading center for goods from both the West and East.

18. **Bronze and early Iron Age Scandinavians used large oared vessels to sail the coasts of the Baltic and North Seas.** These ships would later form the basis for the design of the famous Viking sailing ships.

19. **Ancient Swedish folklore included stories about trolls who lived underneath bridges and mountains** and superstitions such as avoiding walking under ladders dating back to at least 1000 CE.

20. **Prehistoric Swedes had a great understanding of astronomy and tracked the movements of stars,** planets, and the moon.

21. **Archaeological finds include rock art that shows images of the sun, the moon, and the stars.**

22. **A number of stone circles have been found in Sweden.** These are thought to have been used for astronomical observations.

23. **Games played in the later part of this period include "knattleikr"** (similar to modern-day hockey) and **"buhurt"** (a type of mock battle), which were played for entertainment or to train warriors.

24. **Prehistoric and Viking Age Swedes believed in a giant world tree called Yggdrasil that connected all the realms of existence.**

25. **Even before the Viking Age, Scandinavians, including Swedes, were carrying out hit-and-run raids along the Baltic and North Sea coasts.** Ship finds and stone carvings in these areas tell us Scandinavians were raiding on a small scale before the Viking Age.

Swedish Viking Age
(800–1050 CE)

This chapter will explore **the fascinating history of the Swedish Viking Age,** ranging from 800 to 1050 CE. From raids on foreign lands to trade networks that extended as far as **North Africa and the Middle East,** we'll discover how **the Vikings navigated the seas** and established settlements in new lands.

26. **Vikings inhabited the regions of Götaland, Svealand, and Norrland;** these regions are now known as modern-day Sweden.

27. **During the era of Viking expansion into Europe,** Swedes played a notable role in trading with other parts of Europe and raiding them for treasure and slaves.

28. **Though many Swedish warriors joined their Norwegian and Danish relatives in raids on western Europe and the British Isles,** most Swedes traded and sometimes raided in the lands of northeastern Europe, as well as today's Russia and Ukraine.

29. **Swedish Vikings also ventured south to Constantinople, the capital of the Byzantine Empire**

30. **Birka near Stockholm is considered one of the most important archaeological sites related to the**

Viking Age due to the abundance of artifacts that have been found there, such as coins and jewelry belonging to merchants from across Scandinavia, other parts of Europe, central Asia, and even China.

31. **Swedish Vikings had a unique style of dress, which became one of the most recognizable symbols associated with Norse culture.**

32. **Vikings often wore jewelry,** such as brooches, beads, and armbands.

33. By the Middle Ages, **Swedish Viking dress had become one of the most recognizable symbols associated with Norse culture.** It was seen as a symbol of strength, power, and wealth.

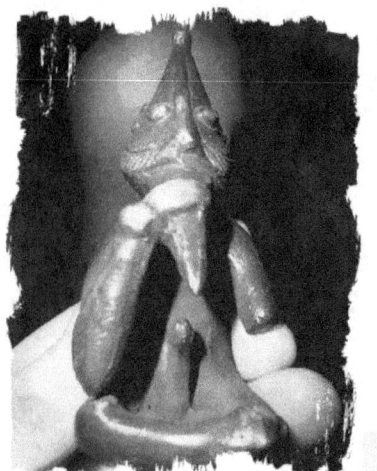

34. **Swedish Vikings engaged in many battles,** some small and some large, such as **the semi-mythical Battle of Bråvalla,** which was fought against Danish Vikings near modern-day Linköpin on the east coast of Sweden. It is thought to have been won by **Swedish warriors despite them being heavily outnumbered.**

35. **The famous runestones found throughout Sweden often tell stories about heroic deeds during this period,** including those related to raiding expeditions abroad or protecting Swedish soil from foreign invaders, such as the Saxons of Germany.

36. **The economy of Viking Age Swedes was based on agriculture supplemented by trading goods like walrus ivory,** seal skins, and furs with other regions, both nearby (Scandinavia) and farther away (like the Middle East).

37. **Swedish Vikings traveled widely across Europe and beyond in search of new lands to settle or trade** opportunities from Scandinavia down to the Mediterranean region and even farther.

38. **The Viking Age saw an increase in population throughout Sweden,** where many areas became more densely populated during this time due to its booming economy fueled by trading abroad.

39. **Most Swedes lived on farms near rural lakes or creeks,** while some larger settlements were along major rivers for easier access between communities using water-based transportation.

40. **Trade routes between Scandinavian countries were well established during this period,** allowing goods like iron ore and timber to be exchanged back and forth quickly without worrying about long overland journeys through potentially hostile territory.

41. **During the Viking Age, Swedish society was divided into classes** with different rights, such as **jarls** (nobles), **bauers** (freemen), and **thralls** (slaves).

42. **The language spoken by Swedish Vikings during this period is known as Old Norse.** Dialects of this language were spoken by Norwegian and Danish Vikings as well. Norse is a Germanic language, and the Scandinavians are considered part of the Germanic group of people.

43. Scandinavian laws from the Viking Age were preserved in later manuscripts and histories written in Latin, giving us insight into how justice was administered and punishment imposed upon criminals during that period in Sweden.

44. Many archaeological findings from this period have been uncovered in Sweden, including jewelry, weapons, and tools, providing us with valuable insight into how the Swedes lived during this time.

45. The Viking Age was a golden era for Swedish artisans, who created intricate designs on objects like swords or wooden staves. **They mainly used animal motifs,** such as dragons or serpents, to decorate them.

46. Swedish Vikings are known to have been very superstitious people. They believed in omens from gods and goddesses, took part in magical rituals, and consulted seers before making important decisions related to battles.

47. Viking-era coins found throughout Scandinavia confirm that there were active trading networks between countries around Europe, providing further evidence of their excellent navigation skills across open seas, even though they lacked the sophisticated equipment of modern vessels.

48. Family and clan ties played an important role in Viking-age Sweden. Married couples were often treated differently than single people for rights or privileges, such as land ownership.

49. Swedish Vikings were known for their love of music and dance, which were often part of religious ceremonies or celebrations after successful raids and battles.

50. Archaeological evidence suggests that Swedish Vikings lived in semi-permanent settlements, with longhouses being the most common type of housing.

51. **Viking burial sites have been discovered throughout Sweden,** revealing notable information on funeral rites, burial customs, and even weapons used by these warriors at the time.

52. In the 830s CE, at the dawn of **the Viking Age, Christianity arrived in Sweden when Saint Ansgar (often called "The Apostle of the North")** brought missionaries from the Frankish Empire, which included most of modern France and parts of Germany. **Christianity would not become the dominant religion of Sweden until the 12th century.**

53. During the Viking Age in **Sweden and Scandinavia, important decisions were often made at the "Thing,"** a meeting of freemen who discussed and often voted on new laws, taxes, criminal penalties, and much more.

54. **Swedish Vikings practiced polygamy and had non-monogamous relationships.** However, these types of relationships were common among certain classes, mainly the jarls (earls). **They could have multiple wives** or concubines without facing legal repercussions.

55. **Norse runes were used by Vikings for communication purposes.** They have been found throughout Scandinavia and even as far south as modern Turkey. **Runes provide valuable insight into their writing system** and how it evolved over the centuries due to contact with other cultures and peoples through trade and other contact.

Medieval Sweden
(1050–1520)

This chapter will explore **the history of medieval Sweden between** 1050 and 1520. Discover how life was in this era for the average Swede and how they interacted with their neighbors. Learn about **the spread of Christianity** and important cultural and political events of the time.

56. **In medieval Sweden, most people made a living through subsistence farming or fishing.**

57. **Christianity was introduced to Sweden in 829 by Ansgar, a Frankish missionary.** Conversion to Christianity in Sweden was smoother than in Norway, but the changes still took more than a century, and the growth of Christianity was not without conflict.

58. **Scandinavia experienced significant population growth during its conversion period from paganism to Christianity.** Better agricultural practices and greater knowledge on many subjects passed from the Catholic Church to the Swedish people, which encouraged the growth of and trust in the church and its faith.

59. **During medieval times, Swedish law was based mainly on ancient Germanic customs and traditions written** down in legal provincial codes called Landskapslagar.

60. Beginning in 1274, **there were attempts at creating a unified kingdom with common laws using Landskapslagar and King Erik IX's Law.**

61. **Throughout much of medieval Swedish history, the most powerful political institution was the Riksrådet** (Royal Council), which consisted of representatives from each province. The Riksrådet had a significant influence on foreign policy and taxation.

62. **During this period, the Hanseatic League, a league of merchant guilds based on the European North Sea and Baltic coasts,** with its most important centers in today's Germany, played an important role in Sweden's economic growth.

63. **The Hanseatic League also became involved in Swedish politics,** influencing the election of kings and gaining privileges within certain regions, such as Gotland, Kalmar, and Visby.

64. **The 13th century endured frequent outbreaks of the plague. Known as the Black Death,** it caused a significant population decline throughout Sweden and Europe.

65. **Several monasteries were founded between 1050 and 1520.** They provided education for both boys and girls who would otherwise not have had access to it due to their socioeconomic status.

66. **The first university in Sweden was Uppsala University,** which was founded in 1477. Uppsala University is still in operation today.

67. **During the Middle Ages, most Swedes didn't travel very far from their homes. Owning a horse,** not to mention a wagon or carriage, was something only nobles and rich merchants could afford.

68. **Early forms of banking were in use during this period.** A system known as **Sänkförsäljning** was introduced, which allowed merchants to sell their goods on credit.

69. **The Swedish language was still significantly influenced by Old Norse at this time,** although several words were replaced due to contact with other languages, such as German and Latin.

70. **Sweden experienced several wars during the medieval period, including the Engelbrekt Rebellion against the Danish king of Sweden** in 1434/35. The people rebelled against harsh taxes and the king's strict rule. The rebellion paved the way for the Swedish War of Independence in the 1520s.

71. **During medieval times, warfare between rival provinces was commonplace within Sweden.** Sweden often engaged in wars against other countries, such as Denmark, Russia, and Norway.

72. **Medieval Sweden saw a rise in literacy rates due to increased access to education.**

73. **Women played an active role in society during this period through their participation in trade or ownership of businesses.** Although higher-class women were expected to stay out of public life, they often played a major role in politics behind the scenes.

74. Between 1350 and 1520, **the construction of large structures, such as churches, castles, and fortifications, took place on a large scale.**

75. **Many works from this period have been preserved, including wall paintings at the Västerås Cathedral** dating back to 1490 and sculptures from Linköping Cathedral built between 1360 and 1400.

76. **The oldest surviving manuscript written in Swedish dates back to around 1320 and is called the Eric Chronicle** (Erikskrönikan in Swedish). This historical and legendary work focuses on the history of Sweden, from its legendary early kings to the author's contemporary period. It encompasses both factual historical accounts and legendary or mythological narratives.

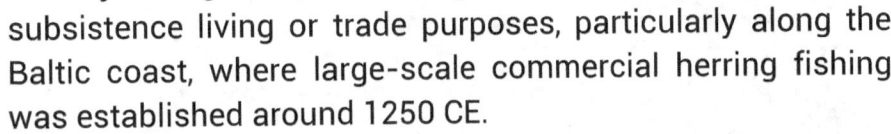

77. **Fishing was an integral activity during this period,** with many people relying on it for subsistence living or trade purposes, particularly along the Baltic coast, where large-scale commercial herring fishing was established around 1250 CE.

78. **Medieval Swedish literature focused mainly on religious themes,** although secular narratives began emerging toward the end of the 15th century.

79. **During the Middle Ages, Swedish coinage was significantly influenced by German and Dutch coins** used in trade throughout northern Europe.

80. Like the Vikings, **medieval Swedes used a variety of currencies,** including some foreign currencies. The use of gold coins was largely limited to royalty and nobility.

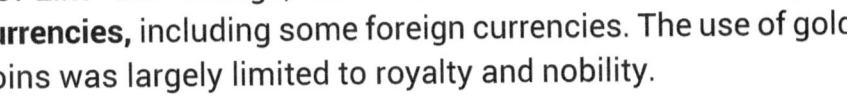

81. **The primary form of entertainment at the time was traditional folk music. In Sweden,** folk music is rich and diverse, with various regional styles and a vast repertoire of traditional tunes and songs. Religious music was also popular, especially at court and on holidays.

82. **Following Christianization, medieval Sweden saw the introduction of new religious holidays,** such as Christmas and Easter. These were celebrated according to pagan traditions, such as **Yule** or **Valborgsmässoafton** (Walpurgis Night).

83. **The University of Uppsala,** Sweden's oldest university, was founded during this period in 1477.

84. In 1527, **the Protestant Reformation began in Sweden,** which saw a shift away from traditional Catholicism. **The Reformation led to increased literacy rates** and the spread of knowledge throughout society due to the publication of the Bible in Swedish by Protestant leaders.

85. **Witch hunts became more common during this period,** with many people, especially women, being accused or tried for witchcraft. **Witchcraft, in the medieval Scandinavian sense,** mostly refers to people practicing old pagan ways or professing a belief in the old gods. Some even suffered death sentences due to superstition and lack of understanding regarding natural phenomena, such as illness.

Kalmar Union
(1397–1523)

This chapter will explore **the history of the Kalmar Union,** which lasted from 1397 to 1523. Discover **how this union formed, its key figures and events,** and its lasting effects on modern Europe today.

86. **The Kalmar Union was a union between three kingdoms: Denmark, Norway, and Sweden.**

87. **The Kalmar Union started in 1397 after Margaret I of Denmark married Haakon VI of Norway.** Haakon died in 1380, and Margaret eventually became the leader of all three countries.

88. **Margaret's reign was disturbed by the rise of an impostor claiming to be her son,** who had allegedly been poisoned by agents of the Hanseatic League of German traders.

89. **The False Olaf scandal rocked the Kalmar Union for a time, as he bore a resemblance to the dead prince.** He was executed for trying to usurp the throne in 1402.

90. **Today's queen of Denmark chose the name Margaret** when she was crowned as a sign of respect to a very influential but much-overlooked queen. She has been queen since 1972.

91. **The union lasted, at least in name, for 126 years** before ending in 1559 with the death of King Christian II.

92. **During this period, people from each country spoke different languages, mainly Danish, Norwegian, and Swedish.**

93. In 1440, **Christopher of Bavaria became king of Denmark.** However, he did not inherit Norway and Sweden at this time.

94. In 1441, **Christopher of Bavaria became the king of Sweden.** When he died without a direct heir, Charles VIII was elected king. He became the king of Denmark a year later.

95. Although **Denmark, Sweden, and Norway were part of the Kalmar Union,** the three were legally separate countries and did not always share the same ruler.

96. **The Kalmar Union's main purpose was to keep peace between the three countries** and defend them from foreign enemies, such as the Hanseatic League, Russia, and the Teutonic Knights.

97. **The Kalmar Union allowed for more trade between the Scandinavian nations,** which increased their wealth and power.

98. In 1520, **Christian II of Denmark declared himself "King of All Scandinavia" after being elected by the nobility,** but this decision caused a lot of controversy since it threatened to dissolve each country's independence within the union.

99. **Christian and many Swedish nobles,** both for and against him, fought a civil war in Sweden. He responded with a massacre known as **the Stockholm Bloodbath.**

100. **Christian II was eventually overthrown by the man who would become Frederick I of Denmark.** Frederick was allied with the most powerful Swedish noble, Gustav Vasa, who became the first king of a unified Sweden in 1523.

101. **The union was finally dissolved in 1523 when Gustav I Vasa became king of Sweden** and separated it from Denmark-Norway.

102. **The Kalmar Union is one of the earliest examples of a unified government between multiple countries,** paving the way for other unions, such as the European Union.

103. During its time, **the Kalmar Union created cultural ties that still exist today.** Swedish people have adopted many Danish words into their language, while both Norwegians and Swedes use some Old Norwegian dialects to communicate with each other.

104. **The influence of the Kalmar Union extended beyond Europe.** Several explorers sponsored by Christian I set sail around 1480 to find new lands.

105. **One of the most famous explorers sponsored by him was Didrik Pining.** Pining was a German explorer who was commissioned by the king to find a new route to Asia. Pining sailed to Greenland in 1472, and he might have even reached mainland North America.

End of Danish Rule
(1660)

Though today they're separate countries, Denmark and Sweden were one until 1523. However, **Denmark retained control of much of southern Sweden** until 1660. This section examines their relationship after **the Kalmar Union** and how the Swedes finally broke free.

106. **Denmark controlled southern Sweden for over a century after Gustav Vasa became king of Sweden.**

107. **Christian IV established a standing** (always on duty) army in 1614 and introduced regular taxes on land, income, and alcohol. **Some of the Danish kings' laws and reforms caused resentment among the Swedes** still under Danish control in southern Sweden.

108. **King Frederik III pursued foreign policy initiatives like waging war against Sweden** from 1643 to 1645 and forming alliances with England and Holland.

109. **This period saw many notable advancements,** including improvements in agriculture techniques, such as crop rotation systems and the use of fertilizers. **There were also advances in architecture,** like Baroque-style buildings and the development of schools and universities.

110. **The Danish conflict with Sweden was fought in four phases: the Northern Seven Years' War** (1563–1570), **the Kalmar War** (1611–1613), **the Dano-Swedish War** (1658–1660), and **the Scanian War** (1675–1679).

111. **The Treaty of Roskilde in 1658 ceded Danish territories to Sweden,** although it did not stop the fighting.

112. In 1659, **Sweden attacked Copenhagen, the capital of Denmark-Norway.** The Danes, with the help of the Dutch, were victorious.

113. **During the many conflicts of this period, there was an influx of Dutch and German merchants into Swedish cities, such as Malmö and Stockholm,** which increased international trading opportunities for Sweden's economy.

114. **The Danes were finally driven out of southern Sweden** in 1660 after **the Dano-Swedish War.**

115. **The end of Danish rule over Sweden meant that Sweden was a fully independent country.** By the 17th century, it was considered one of the greatest powers in Europe.

Protestant Reformation in Sweden
(1527–1660)

The Protestant Reformation in Sweden was a crucial time for the country and the course of Swedish history. In this chapter, explore interesting facts about this momentous event and its influence on religion, politics, culture, and more.

116. **The Protestant Reformation in Sweden began in 1527 after King Gustav Vasa** took control of the country in 1523.

117. **It was part of a widespread movement** that influenced all of Europe during this time period.

118. **The main figure behind the Swedish Reformation was Olaus Petri** (1493–1552), **a German-born priest who introduced Lutheran teachings to Sweden from Germany and Denmark** after the Reformation began in Germany in 1517.

119. **Petri helped translate the Bible into Swedish. This Bible** is called **the Gustav Vasa Bible.**

120. **Olaus's brother Laurentius** (1499–1573) also **helped spread Lutheranism throughout Sweden** with his writings. He inspired many Swedes to convert to Protestantism.

121. In 1544, **under the leadership of Gustav Vasa, Sweden made Lutheranism the state religion.** For many years, Catholics in Sweden were persecuted, made to convert, and worshiped in hiding.

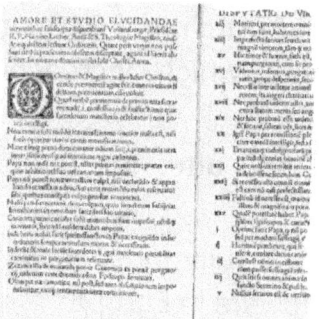

122. In 1617, **King Gustavus II Adolphus adopted the Heidelberg Catechism from Germany.** It serves as one of the main documents guiding **Lutheran belief in Sweden today.**

123. **The Reformation also brought about changes in education.** More universities were created for the study of theology and literature.

124. **Hospitals, orphanages, and schools were established** to support society's less fortunate members.

125. **Religious art was featured in churches throughout Sweden,** though religious paintings of this time emphasized stories from the Bible, **not images of saints and popes**, which was popular in Catholic Europe.

126. **The Reformation eventually led to greater freedom of religion,** allowing people to worship freely without fear of persecution from their peers or leaders, though it was a slow, evolving process.

127. **It is believed that prior to this time, most Swedes had been Catholic,** but few remained so by the end of 1660, which is considered the end of the Swedish Reformation.

128. **During this period, women gradually gained more rights in public life, but the changes in religion diminished the role of women in the church.** For instance, abbeys were abolished, ending many women's roles as nuns.

129. **In 1958, Sweden was one of the first Lutheran countries to allow female pastors.**

130. **Lutheran churches began to appear all over Sweden, replacing Catholic** ones and becoming part of the landscape. Many still stand today as a testament to this influential era in Sweden's history.

131. **Throughout northern and central Europe, including Scandinavia, reforms and increased literacy influenced the Scientific Revolution,** leading to inventions like clocks, new ways of farming, and improved navigation techniques.

132. During this era, **Sweden developed a strong maritime industry that allowed it to become a naval power in the Baltic and North Seas; this** was partly due **to King Gustav II Adolph's naval reforms** (r. 1611–1632).

133. **Lutheranism helped advance literacy throughout Sweden,** with people encouraged to learn how to read and write so they could study scripture for themselves.

134. **Protestant values were embraced by Swedish society during this period,** especially a strong work ethic, thriftiness, and self-sufficiency—all qualities needed for success at sea or on land.

135. People during **this time were encouraged to think independently and make their own decisions about religious matters.** This was a key factor in why Lutheranism became so popular.

Rise and Fall of the Swedish Empire
(1611–1721)

The Swedish Empire was one of the most influential and powerful forces in early modern Europe. This chapter will explore the fascinating history of this empire, from its rise to its fall.

136. **The Swedish Empire began in 1611 when King Gustavus II Adolphus became the ruler of Sweden.**

137. During this period, **Sweden was one of the most powerful countries in Europe** and had a large amount of territory in and influence on other countries around it.

138. By 1721, **the Swedish Empire included parts of modern-day Norway, Finland, Estonia, Latvia, Russia, and Germany.**

139. **During King Gustavus II Adolphus's rule (1611–1632), he increased the power and size of Sweden's military forces,** which helped to rapidly expand the empire's boundaries through conquest or alliance with other nations.

140. **King Charles (Karl) XII led an aggressive foreign policy during his reign from 1697 to 1718. He invaded Russia,** which eventually led to his downfall due to poor strategic decisions, resulting in heavy losses for Swedish forces against Russia and other enemies.

141. **The Russian Army was much larger than the Swedish Army,** and the Russian terrain was difficult to navigate. Charles XII was eventually defeated at **the Battle of Poltava** in 1709, and he was forced to flee to Turkey.

142. **Charles XII remained in Turkey for several years, and he refused to make peace with Russia.** This allowed Russia to regroup and launch a counter-offensive against Sweden. By the time **Charles XII returned to Sweden in 1718,** Sweden was already in decline.

143. **The Swedish economy was heavily reliant on foreign trade and was affected by war,** famine, and plague during the late 17th century, which led to a decline in its population and its military strength, at least compared to other European nations at that time.

144. In 1648, **Sweden was one of the signatories to the Peace of Westphalia, the treaty ending the Thirty Years' War.**

145. **Sweden's decline was caused in part by the Great Northern War,** which lasted from 1700 to 1721 and pitted **Sweden against a coalition led by Russia, Denmark-Norway, and Saxony.** This conflict saw Sweden decline in power and eventually lose many territories, including **Estonia, Latvia, and parts of Germany, such as Pomerania.**

146. **When King Charles XII died** while fighting against Norway, it caused a succession crisis since no clear successor was chosen by the nobles who were ruling over Sweden.

147. **The period known as the Age of Liberty followed after King Charles XII died in 1718.** No monarch ruled over Sweden. Instead, the nation was governed by a **parliamentary system called Riksdag,** which had representatives from all classes.

148. **The Swedish Empire survived several wars throughout its existence, including the Thirty Years' War** (1618–1648) and **the Great Northern War** (1700–1721). **The Treaty of Nystad ended the Great Northern War** and ended the Swedish Empire's power.

149. **The Swedish Empire was a major player in European politics** and had alliances with England, France, and the Netherlands. Its main rival during this period was Denmark-Norway, which also wanted to expand its influence.

150. **The Swedish Army relied heavily on the conscription of men from each social class throughout its existence.**

151. At sea, **the Swedish Empire had one of the largest fleets operating in Europe** due to its large merchant marine industry.

152. **The Swedish economy grew significantly during this era,** mainly through foreign trade. **Sweden exported timber and iron ore;** these resources allowed it to become more powerful militarily compared to neighboring countries like Russia or Prussia, which did not have access to the same type of materials.

153. During its peak in 1658, Sweden was the third-largest country in Europe after Russia and Spain.

154. The end of the Swedish Empire marked a new beginning for Sweden's development into the modern-day nation we know today, with democratic institutions, **a strong economy based on exports,** and a welfare state providing equal opportunities for people living there.

155. Sweden was one of the first European countries to abolish serfdom in 1810, meaning peasants who worked on estates owned by aristocrats no longer had any obligation towards them and could live freely like any other person during that period; **this helped increase social mobility in society significantly,** compared before when people's lives were determined based on class status.

Queen Christina
(1626–1689)

Christina of Sweden was a brilliant and controversial figure who reigned as queen of Sweden from 1632 to 1654. She was the first female monarch in Sweden and one of the most learned women of her time. Let's look at five interesting facts about this influential ruler.

156. **Christina was born on December** 18th, 1626, at the royal palace in Stockholm, Sweden. She was the only child of **King Gustav II Adolf and Queen Maria Eleonora.**

157. **She was educated as a royal male would have been**, which means she learned how to fence and shoot.

158. **Christina was crowned queen at the age of six after her father was killed in battle in 1632.** She was the first female monarch in Sweden.

159. **Christina had a habit of wearing pants and men's outfits** at a time when that was essentially forbidden to most women.

160. **Some believed she was a lesbian.** In truth, historians believe that, for a time at least, Christina was in love with another woman.

161. **Christina was a brilliant and well-educated woman.** She spoke several languages, including Latin, Greek, and French. She was also a patron of the arts and sciences.

162. In 1654, **Christina abdicated the Swedish throne and converted to Catholicism.** She moved to Rome, where she lived the rest of her life.

163. **Though many initially believed she had converted to Catholicism** to become a more pious person, she was famous in Rome for her parties and lavish spending.

164. **Christina died on April 19th, 1689, at the age of sixty-two.** She was buried in St. Peter's Basilica in Rome.

165. **Queen Christina has inspired many books, operas, plays, and movies.** The 1933 film **Queen Christina, starring Greta Garbo,** is a highly fictionalized account of her life. **Jacopo Foroni's opera, Cristina, regina di Svezia,** is based on her abdication of the throne.

The Age of Liberty
(1718–1772)

This chapter will explore the remarkable Age of Liberty in Sweden. Examine notable facts about **this time and how it shaped Swedish culture, politics, and society.** From the development of unprecedented **freedom of speech** to new economic policies that transformed the industry, we will discover what made this era so significant in Sweden's history.

166. **The Age of Liberty took off after the Great Northern War,** which ended in 1721.

167. After **King Charles XII's death in 1718, no single ruler had full control over the country for fifty-four years.**

168. During this period, **reforms were enacted that gave merchants and peasant farmers more rights** and influence in their country.

169. **There were four "Estates" or classes** during this period: **the clergy, nobility, burghers** (merchants), and **peasants** (farmers).

170. **The clergy and the nobility had more power than the burghers and the peasants** and influenced them greatly. However, all four estates had to agree on laws before they could be passed. This meant the peasants had a say in the government, even though they were the lowest estate.

171. **During the Age of Liberty, Anders Celsius, a Swedish astronomer and physicist, developed the Celsius temperature scale,** which is still used today. He also made significant contributions to the study of **optics and astronomy.**

172. **Carl Linnaeus** (1707–1778), **a Swedish botanist, developed the binomial nomenclature system for classifying organisms.** He is considered the father of modern taxonomy.

173. **Ulrika Pasch** (1735–1796) **was a Swedish artist** who was the first woman to be accepted **into the Royal Swedish Academy of Arts.** Her brother was also a member, but he, like all male members, received a stipend. She did not.

174. **Eve Ekeblad, an agronomist who developed a method of creating flour from potatoes,** was the first woman to be elected to the Swedish Academy of Sciences.

175. **Ekeblad also developed a newer, faster, and more efficient way of distilling alcohol from potatoes.** She helped improve vodka production.

176. **Christopher Polhem (1661–1751) made significant contributions to the fields of engineering, mechanics, and mining.**

177. **The first newspaper in Sweden was published in 1645,** which allowed people to learn news happening around the country and, occasionally, other parts of Europe and the world

178. **Trade increased significantly between Sweden and nations like England, Spain, France, and Portugal.**

179. **The economy improved with new industries such as mining, ironworks,** and other manufacturing businesses beginning to develop throughout much of Sweden.

180. **During the Age of Liberty**, Sweden saw its first steam engine in 1753. It was used to pump water out of mines.

181. **Art flourished during this period.** Portraits became popular among the wealthy, and several grand buildings were built in cities.

182. **Carl Gustaf Pilo (1711-1793) was one of the leading artists of the Age of Liberty,** introducing the rococo style to Sweden and painting many powerful people.

183. **Famous composer Carl Michael Bellman (1740–1795)** wrote several songs about drinking during this time. These songs are still widely enjoyed today.

184. **King Gustav III restored the absolute monarchy in 1772 by overthrowing the parliament with a coup d'état,** which ended the Age of Liberty.

185. **The Age of Liberty in Sweden was an integral part of the country's history,** as it laid the foundation for its modernization and growth.

Gustav III's Coup D'état and Rule
(1772–1792)

This chapter will delve into the fascinating history of Gustav III's reign. Explore interesting facts about the coup, and learn more about the consequences of this pivotal event.

186. **In August 1772, Gustav III staged a coup d'état and seized power from the Riksdag** (parliament) **in Stockholm.**

187. **The coup was secretly planned with the help of foreign allies** and his closest friends at court.

188. **His reign is known as the Gustavian era in Sweden because he introduced many reforms that notably improved life in Sweden** during this period, including abolishing certain capital punishments, establishing freedom of speech and press (provided it didn't question his rule), reforming taxation laws, and creating new universities across the nation.

189. **He also reduced the national debt by two-thirds while increasing pensions for retired soldiers and families** who lost family members due to war or sickness caused by poverty.

190. From 1772 to 1788, **Gustav allied Sweden with Russia and its empress, Catherine the Great.**

191. **When the alliance came apart in 1788, Sweden and Russia** went to war, which ended in 1790, with their borders remaining the same as before.

192. **Gustav encouraged Swedish industry by encouraging and supporting the building of factories to trade** with other countries in Europe and the Americas.

193. **Some of Gustav's reforms included the abolition of guilds.** Guilds were organizations of merchants and craftsmen that had a monopoly on certain trades. **Gustav III believed the abolition of guilds would free up the market** and allow for more competition.

194. **Gustav III abolished most tariffs and restrictions on trade.** This made it easier for Swedish businesses to export their goods and import raw materials.

195. **Gustav III invited foreign investors to come to Sweden and set up businesses.** He also offered them tax breaks and other incentives.

196. **Gustav III was a great patron of the arts and literature.** He established the Royal Academy of Fine Arts, which still exists today.

197. **Gustav III's reforms caused tension between him and some members of the nobility who disagreed with them,** leading to his assassination in 1792. He was attending a masquerade ball at Stockholm's Royal Opera House when he was shot.

198. **Gustav's coup d'état is important because it allowed Gustav III** to have more power than any other king before him, allowing for more notable and rapid reforms that helped improve life in Sweden.

199. **Gustav III only had one son: Gustav IV Adolf. Gustav IV Adolf was deposed** in 1809 and exiled from Sweden. He never had any children, so **the throne passed to his uncle, Charles XIII.**

200. **Charles XIII was childless, so he adopted Jean-Baptiste Bernadotte, a French general** who had fought for **Napoleon Bonaparte.** Bernadotte became **King Charles XIV John of Sweden in 1818.**

201. **Gustav III's reign is often referred to as the Swedish Enlightenment** because of his promotion of intellectual and cultural pursuits.

202. **Gustav's coup is seen as a turning point in Swedish history** because it marked a period of notable progress for the country compared to previous absolute monarchies that had restricted freedom and reforms.

203. **The coup has been remembered through artwork, books,** and plays about this period, which have become part of Swedish culture.

204. **The legacy of Gustav III's era can still be seen today** in many institutions that still exist, such as the Royal Academy of Fine Arts.

205. **This event also inspired other countries to implement similar political changes during their revolutions.**

Reforms and Political Changes in Sweden
(1792–1809)

This chapter will explore the intriguing reforms and political changes that took place in Sweden from 1792 to 1809. Delve into notable facts about Swedish society during this period, including their successes and failures in politics, culture, economy, and everyday life.

206. **In 1792, Sweden changed from an absolute monarchy to a constitutional monarchy.** Under the constitutional monarchy, the monarch had less power.

207. **Though Gustav III had begun his reign as a somewhat enlightened monarch,** he became increasingly autocratic.

208. **Gustav III was assassinated in 1792 by a disgruntled military officer,** but by this time, many Swedes had had enough of the absolute monarchy.

209. **In 1798, Sweden abolished censorship laws that had been imposed by the previous kings,** allowing for greater freedom of expression within the country.

210. **The new constitution, known as the Instrument of Government of 1809,** established principles of freedom of speech and freedom of the press in Sweden.

211. **Citizens had more rights than before,** including freedom of assembly without permission from authorities

212. The 1809 **Instrument of Government was replaced with the 1974 Instrument of Government,** which ensured democracy and the people's rights.

213. **Equality before the law became part of Swedish society in 1809.** All people were equal regardless of class or gender except for voting rights; only men could vote at that time. However, **although all people were equal before the law,** it would be years before this became a recognized fact.

214. A modern system for taxation was introduced in 1798, including taxes on tobacco products and alcohol, which helped pay off state debt faster than before.

215. The Swedish banking system was reformed and modernized in 1798, which helped stimulate economic growth.

216. During this time, education became more available in the countryside, especially regarding farming and animal husbandry, which led to an increased population and less hunger.

217. Though the death penalty was in effect in Sweden until 1910, torture as a legal means of criminal investigation was officially halted in 1772. Many other European countries still used torture in the late 18th century.

218. On top of this, the king officially lost power over the government by giving up his right to appoint ministers who would serve him directly instead of having them appointed by Parliament through a majority vote.

219. All property-owning men over twenty-five years old became eligible to vote in 1809, except that non-nobles were not able to vote for the upper house of the Riksdag.

220. Universal suffrage (equal voting rights for all citizens) **was introduced in 1921, granting women the right to vote.**

221. The Riksdag became more powerful, which allowed Parliament to control taxation laws and military spending without the king's permission or oversight.

222. Workers were granted better working conditions. They could work fewer hours a week, and new regulations protected them from exploitation through dangerous labor practices, such as child labor.

223. Reforms did not completely eliminate the exploitation of workers. Child labor was still widespread, and many workers were subjected to dangerous working conditions.

224. In 1812, a law to introduce conscription (drafting citizens into military service) was passed but only applied to younger men aged twenty to twenty-seven who had enough money to pay for their uniforms and equipment. This meant that the poor were effectively excluded from military service, which is usually not the case.

225. Lastly, the Supreme Court (Högsta domstolen) was formed in 1789, allowing citizens to appeal if they felt justice wasn't served in the lower courts.

Napoleonic Wars
(1803–1815)

This chapter will explore **the history of Sweden and how it was impacted by the Napoleonic Wars.** From **naval battles with Britain** to diplomatic relationships with France, learn interesting facts about one of the most important periods in Swedish history.

226. **The Napoleonic Wars were a series of wars fought between France and various European countries from 1803 to 1815.**

227. **Sweden was part of coalitions against France from 1803 to 1807** and again after 1813.

228. **In 1806, Swedish troops fought alongside Russian forces in Prussia,** forcing Napoleon's army out of Berlin and defeating them at Jena-Auerstedt. However, the coalition forces were unable to capitalize on their victory.

229. **Napoleon regrouped his forces and defeated the coalition at the Battle of Friedland in June 1809.** This forced the coalition to sue for peace, and Sweden was eventually forced to cede Finland to Russia due to a complicated shift in alliances.

230. **After the assassination of Gustav IV Adolphus, Charles XIII became king. Sweden** became a reluctant ally of Napoleonic France.

231. **Swedes played a role in defeating Napoleon at Leipzig** (1813). Ten thousand Swedish troops joined in heavy fighting against 250,000 French soldiers until the French finally capitulated on October 19th.

232. **In addition to battles on land, many naval engagements occurred around Scandinavia** throughout the conflict, with British and French fleets operating off its coasts.

233. **A combined Anglo-English fleet defeated the united Danes and Norwegians** twice at sea near the Danish capital of Copenhagen. This resulted in Denmark giving Norway to Sweden and having to join the alliance against Napoleon.

234. **During this period, many Swedes were conscripted to fight for their country** abroad on the side of the English or at home, but some chose to join Napoleon's forces as mercenaries instead.

235. **The French invasion of Russia in 1812 was one of the most damaging events for both sides.** Thousands were killed, and great destruction and economic disruption took place. It affected Sweden due to its proximity to Russia.

236. **Many famous Swedes fought during this time, including King Charles XIII, Carl Johan Adlercreutz,** and **the "king-elect," Marshal Jean Bernadotte,** who later became King Charles XIV John of Sweden in 1818.

237. **Perhaps the most famous Swedish military commander was Carl Johan Adlercreutz,** who fought against both **the Russians and the French**. Adlercreutz's most famous victory came at **the Battle of Jutas in 1808**. The Swedes were outnumbered by **the Russians,** but Adlercreutz was able to outmaneuver **the Russian forces and inflict a decisive defeat on them.** This victory helped to turn the tide of **the Finnish War in favor of Sweden.**

238. **Adlercreutz also played a key role in the Battle of Leipzig in 1813.** By then, **the Swedes were part of the Sixth Coalition,** which was opposed to Napoleon

239. **The Napoleonic Wars had a notable impact on Swedish politics and society,** with many reforms occurring throughout this period, such as the modernization of its military forces and the naming of a new king. **This new king was actually a Frenchman who had been one of Napoleon's early supporters and generals.**

240. **When Jean Bernadotte became king, he took the name Charles XIV John and instituted Sweden's** most important foreign policy decision until 2023. He declared that Sweden would be a neutral country and stay out of overseas wars.

241. **Sweden's neutrality policy continued until Russia's invasion of Ukraine in 2022** when it applied to join NATO. The neutrality policy was central to Swedish military, political, and economic policies for over two hundred years.

242. **Two major battles were fought in Finland, which was Swedish territory,** during this time: **the Battle of Jutas and the Battle of Sävar. Jutas was a Swedish victory.** The Battle of Sävar saw Sweden lose to Russia.

243. **Many Swedes perished during this conflict due to famine or disease associated with fighting** for extended periods of time abroad or within their borders.

244. **Sweden's involvement in the Napoleonic Wars** left it heavily indebted due to its military expenditure during that period.

245. **During this era, there was a rise in patriotism within Sweden,** as citizens felt they had been instrumental in liberating Europe from French rule.

Union with Norway
(1814–1905)

This chapter will explore the exciting history of Sweden's union with Norway. We'll uncover fascinating facts about this period in **Swedish history**, including how it came into being and the impact of the union on politics, the economy, and culture.

246. **The union officially formed in 1814 after the first defeat of Napoleon in the Napoleonic Wars.** The king of Denmark-Norway was forced to cede Norway to Sweden, creating **the United Kingdoms of Sweden and Norway.**

247. **The union was a personal union, which means the two countries shared the same king but had separate governments.** The king of Sweden was also the king of Norway, and he appointed a governor-general to represent him there. However, **Norway had its own parliament,** its own laws, and its own currency.

248. **King Charles XIII ruled over both nations during this time, a period known as Unionstiden in Swedish,** which means "the Union Time." However, for the most part, Norway ran its own affairs.

249. **During this period, each country had a government responsible for internal affairs,** although foreign policy remained under joint control by the two governments alongside their monarchs in charge, thus creating a unique government structure at that time.

250. **Economic cooperation increased significantly during this period, especially within the banking and trading sectors,** allowing Norway to become more integrated into the European market.

251. Even though **the two countries maintained distinct parliaments,** they were both represented in a joint parliament from 1891 onward. **They also had shared government ministries and agencies,** such as defense and foreign affairs.

252. **This period is known as a time of economic growth, especially in Sweden.** Shipping, banking, timber, and mining led the way, helping to create numerous new jobs.

253. In 1889, **Norway's independence within the union was established when it adopted its own constitution separate from that of Sweden's,** although it was still tied to Sweden through a king, a shared currency, and a united foreign policy.

254. Norwegian currency changed from the Danish kroner, which was used before the union with Sweden, **to the Swedish krona** (or kroner) in 1875.

255. The Norwegian language became official within public institutions in Norway, replacing Danish, which had been the language of government and commerce during Danish rule.

256. Norway benefited from the union, gaining access to Swedish resources and markets, which allowed the Norwegians to develop their economy and industries.

257. For much of the Swedish-Norwegian union, foreign affairs were a bone of contention, as both countries had differing interests.

258. The union with Norway was seen by many Norse as an opportunity for greater integration into European politics while allowing them more freedom from Denmark's control.

259. As part of the terms set out with the help of Napoleon, Sweden gave Finland to Russia in 1809 after suffering a defeat in the short Finnish War.

260. The union with Norway allowed for a better division of labor between the two nations and made it possible to exploit resources more efficiently than before, especially within fisheries and timber production.

261. Tensions started rising between Sweden and Norway over various issues, such as taxation. In 1905, the union ended, and each country became independent again.

262. Following the dissolution in 1905, Norway became fully independent while maintaining close ties (especially economically) with Sweden.

263. Despite their shared history, some cultural differences between Swedes and Norwegians can be seen nowadays through language, cuisine, or customs.

264. Although not everyone in Sweden or Norway supported the union at the beginning, it was eventually seen as a necessary step that allowed for greater cooperation between both nations and ultimately made them stronger.

265. Today, this period is remembered by many Swedes and Norwegians, especially within literature and popular culture.

The New Era of Swedish Politics
(1905–1914)

This chapter will explore the complex political landscape of Sweden during the period between 1905 and 1914. Examine interesting facts about this era, including how politics was shaped by social and economic changes and international developments in Europe.

266. **The new era of Swedish politics began when Sweden created new voting rules** in 1905. In 1909, all men over twenty-five could vote, and women were allowed to vote in local elections (they could not vote in national elections until 1921).

267. **During this era, Sweden saw many changes in government,** with different parties controlling Parliament at various times, as well as multiple prime ministers.

268. **Women began to affect the political life of Sweden during this era.** Swedish women have since played a huge political role in the country for decades, and **Magdalena Andersson became Sweden's first female prime minister** in 2021.

269. **The most successful political party during this era was the Liberal Party,** which won four out of five elections between 1910 and 1914, with **Karl Staaff becoming prime minister** in 1905 and again in 1911.

270. In 1906, **a new law gave workers the right to form trade unions and bargain collectively,** which improved working conditions across Sweden.

271. In 1919, **Sweden became one of the first European countries to introduce an eight-hour workday for all employees.**

272. **This new era of Swedish politics also saw a rise in science and technology,** with the creation of many new industries and increased investment in education.

273. **Sweden slowly converted to electricity during this period,** which began to bring modern comforts, such as electric stoves, washing machines, and cars, into homes across the country, though it was a slow process, especially in the countryside.

274. **This era ended when World War I broke out in 1914,** leading most countries to stop focusing on domestic issues.

275. **This era of Swedish politics is remembered as a significant step forward for democracy in Scandinavia** by introducing more expansive voting rights and helping establish stronger workers' rights.

Swedish Neutrality during WWI
(1914–1918)

Did you know Sweden remained neutral during World War I? Uncover facts about how this small Scandinavian nation maintained its independence and remained neutral throughout the war.

276. **Neutral Sweden stayed out of World War I and did not take sides with Germany,** Austria-Hungary, Russia, Britain, or France.

277. **The Swedish government wanted to keep the country safe from being invaded** by any foreign powers during this period, so it kept to its policy of neutrality while still arming itself.

278. **During WWI, Sweden traded with both sides,** selling items like iron ore and timber while buying food for their people and military supplies for defensive purposes like ammunition and raw materials.

279. **Due to Sweden's location, it mostly traded with Germany.**

280. **Sweden allowed German submarines to dock in its ports,** giving them access to fuel needed for their operations elsewhere in Europe during WWI. Other neutral countries like

Norway protested this act because they were concerned about this impacting their safety and security. **Sweden allowed this to happen because it was afraid that Germany, which was much stronger, might attack.**

281. **The Swedes used diplomatic channels throughout the war to ensure they could remain a neutral state and not be dragged into the conflict.**

282. **Though Sweden remained neutral, there were a number of Swedes, many of whom had German ancestry,** who wanted Sweden to aid Germany exclusively. However, the number of people who wanted to send troops to help Germany was small.

283. **The Swedish government was so successful at maintaining neutrality** that no foreign military forces ever invaded its territory during this period.

284. **Sweden's neutrality enabled it to stay out of World War I** while maintaining strong economic ties throughout Europe, ensuring its economy remained healthy despite all the turmoil happening elsewhere.

285. **During WWI, Sweden provided refugee status to more than 500,000 people** from other countries seeking safety, including German and Austrian refugees fleeing their countries' drafts.

286. **The Swedish royal family provided refuge for several political exiles throughout WWI**, including members of the Russian tsar's extended family who fled their homeland after **the Bolshevik Revolution in Russia** in 1917.

287. **Sweden's neutrality allowed the nation to be a mediator during peace negotiations between Germany and Britain on two separate occasions** (1916 and 1918), which helped bring about negotiations that ultimately led toward an armistice signed in November 1918.

288. **Sweden remained neutral even after the war ended, signifying the success of its policy.**

289. **Sweden used its neutrality to strengthen diplomatic ties with other countries,** such as Russia and France, which enabled it to have more influence in international politics in the years after WWI ended.

290. **Sweden's neutrality policy was criticized by many on both sides of the war.** Germany believed Sweden should have sided with it because the countries had historically close ties. The British and French saw Germany as an aggressor that had to be stopped at all costs.

291. **The Swedes provided medical aid and supplies to countries involved in WWI,** demonstrating how they could remain neutral while providing much-needed humanitarian assistance.

292. **Though most Swedes supported neutrality,** there were people who believed their nation needed to enter the war on one side or another.

293. **Swedish neutrality enabled the nation to have access to international funds and loans,** which benefited Sweden since other countries were financially drained due to the war effort.

294. **Sweden maintained strong ties with both sides during World War I,** allowing it to remain neutral yet still be an important player in international politics.

295. **The success of Swedish neutrality during WWI is widely seen as one of its proudest moments in history.** It set up a legacy for future generations who could learn how peaceful diplomacy could be used effectively even amidst a major global conflict.

Swedish Life and Culture between the Wars (1918–1939)

This chapter will explore the turbulent history of Sweden during the interwar period. The world saw some massive changes during this time, **and Sweden definitely felt the impact as well.** Let's look at what happened to Sweden before **the start of World War II.**

296. During the interwar period, **Sweden became one of Europe's wealthiest countries and experienced rapid industrialization.**

297. **The Swedish economy was based on exports,** such as iron ore, paper, textiles, and timber.

298. Though founded in 1889, **the Social Democratic Party** (Sveriges socialdemokratiska arbetareparti, or Socialdemokraterna) won elections in Sweden for the first time in 1932 and remained in power until 1976.

299. **Women made significant strides during this period.** For instance, they were given the right to vote in national elections in 1921. By 1931, more than **50 percent of university teachers were female**, though this figure only includes public universities. Private universities were not required to report statistics.

300. **Though wealthier Swedes had begun to purchase cars,** most people did not own one in 1929. Most people in cities still traveled by streetcar, and businesses used horses and wagons.

301. **Air travel started becoming popular during this period,** with commercial flights offered between Stockholm and Gothenburg in 1928. These flights were operated using German-made Junkers, which could carry up to twelve passengers. Flying on a plane was relatively expensive.

302. **Art Deco became a trendy style in cities like Stockholm and Gothenburg,** reflecting international trends.

303. **Swedish culture saw an explosion of creativity during this period,** with many famous authors such as **Selma Lagerlöf** (The Wonderful Adventures of Nils, 1909 Nobel Prize for Literature) and Hjalmar Söderberg (Martin Birck's Youth and Doktor Glas) writing their masterpieces.

304. **Music flourished with composers like Hugo Alfvén creating works like Swedish Rhapsody No. 1** based on traditional folk music melodies from Sweden and other parts of Scandinavia.

305. In 1909, one of **Europe's first ski resorts opened up at Åre, now a popular destination for skiing enthusiasts globally. Swe**

306. By 1939, **about 90 percent of Swedish households had access to electricity.** About 60 percent of Swedish households had a telephone.

307. **During the interwar period, there were about one million radio receivers in Sweden. Radio was a major source of entertainment and information.**

308. **Cinemas started appearing across cities, and movies from Hollywood made their way into Swedish theaters.**

309. **Sweden also developed its own movie industry. Hollywood superstar Greta Garbo** (1905–1990) was born in Sweden and got her start in the Swedish movie industry.

310. **The interwar period saw a rapid rise in Swedish banks, which helped create a stable economy for the country.** The Swedish economy grew rapidly during the interwar period, which led to an increase in demand for banking services.

Neutrality during WWII
(1939–1945)

Sweden was a neutral country during World War II. In this chapter, we explore how Sweden's neutrality affected its relationship with Germany and other European countries during one of the toughest moments in recorded history.

311. **To maintain its neutral status, Sweden had to accept certain restrictions,** such as trade limitations imposed by Allied forces and the Axis powers during WWII.

312. **While Sweden's military was not as strong as the Allies or Axis**, it was still strong enough to deter an attack. This, combined with Sweden's strategic location and **the diplomatic skills of the Swedish government,** helped the nation maintain its neutrality during World War II.

313. **Sweden allowed German soldiers to move through its territory** on the condition that they refrain from military activities while there.

314. **Some reports indicate that German troops stationed in Norway used Swedish territory for operations against Allied forces** nearby. This information was not widely known until after the war, and it damaged Sweden's reputation as a neutral country.

315. **Despite attempts at maintaining strict rules about entering Swedish borders, there were instances when German troops that entered the country were treated with a certain level of hospitality rather than suspicion.**

316. **The Swedish government provided humanitarian aid to both sides during WWII** by sending food and supplies to prisoner-of-war camps in Germany, Italy, France, and other countries.

317. **Sweden took in about nine thousand Jewish refugees during the war,** including some eight thousand Danish Jews, after the German invasion of Denmark.

318. The Swedes took an active role in negotiating peace treaties between the Allies and Axis forces. For instance, they acted as mediators between Finland and the Soviet Union in 1944, which earned them great respect on an international level.

319. Some argue that Sweden's stance on neutrality wasn't always consistent since there were reports suggesting that its military had plans for operations against Nazi Germany should it ever invade its territory.

320. Sweden provided materials to Germany during the war, such as iron ore and timber, which were essential for their military operations. Germany surrounded Sweden during the war, so the country could not trade with the Allies.

321. There was little internal conflict or violence within Sweden during the war, although the nation was blockaded and accidentally bombed at times.

322. One of the most famous civilians of WWII in Europe was Raoul Wallenberg, a Swedish aristocrat who worked with the Red Cross in Hungary. He is credited with saving the lives of thousands of Hungarian Jews who might have ended up in Auschwitz.

323. Wallenberg disappeared at the end of the war. It wasn't until decades later that it was discovered **the Soviets had captured him** when their troops entered Hungary. They believed he was a spy and sent him to **the Soviet prison camp system,** where he died in 1947 under mysterious circumstances.

324. Despite their neighbors, Denmark and Norway, being invaded, Sweden managed to prevent an invasion and stay neutral.

325. In summary, Sweden's policy of neutrality during WWII was an integral part of its history, as it allowed the Swedes to maintain security while still providing help for those who needed it.

Swedish Free-Market Reform Era
(1939–1976)

This chapter will explore Sweden's free-market reform era. Explore facts about this important period in Swedish economic and social history, including how it transformed the country into one of the most prosperous nations in Europe.

326. **This period saw Sweden become an economic power** worth far more than the size of its population would indicate.

327. **The government implemented policies that reduced taxes on businesses,** eliminated tariffs on imported goods, improved working conditions, and encouraged entrepreneurship by supporting small business owners.

328. **The state provided generous welfare benefits, including universal healthcare,** free education through college-level studies, unemployment insurance, housing subsidies, pension plans, and parental leave for parents working outside the home. It allowed people to enjoy a high-quality life while maintaining social stability even after retirement at an early age.

329. **One reason Sweden was able to provide these social services was its high taxes on individuals.** The top marginal tax rate for individuals in Sweden was 91 percent in 1954.

330. **Swedish taxes are progressive. This means that people who earn more money pay a higher percentage of their income in taxes,** which helps to ensure everyone contributes to the tax system according to their ability to pay.

331. **Tax rates in Sweden began to decline in the late 1960s and 1970s,** but they remained relatively high compared to other countries due to the government's commitment to social welfare programs.

332. The high tax rates in Sweden were a source of controversy during this period. Some people argued they were too high and discouraged people from working hard. Others argued they were necessary to fund the social welfare programs that made Sweden a more equitable society.

333. During this period, Sweden was one of the world's wealthiest countries in GDP (gross domestic product) per capita (person).

334. By the 1970s, 67 percent of **Swedish families owned their own homes compared to just 34 percent at the start of the reform period in 1939.**

335. The reforms also led to increased industrial production, which resulted in higher exports and generated more revenue for the country's economy while helping to reduce joblessness.

336. The unemployment rate in Sweden declined significantly during this period, going from 14.3 percent in 1939 to 2.9 percent in 1976.

337. Social democratic parties were the dominant forces behind many of these free-market reforms. They provided the framework for a strong economy, which, in turn, led to increased standards of living.

338. Sweden benefited from being one of the few European countries not physically damaged by WWII, which, combined with the need for raw materials in war-torn Europe, helped the Swedish economy greatly.

339. In 1960, Sweden joined EFTA (European Free Trade Association), allowing it access to the European market and further strengthening its economic growth.

340. By the late 1970s, **Sweden had established itself as one of Europe's most prosperous nations.**

The Cold War
(1955–1991)

This chapter will explore the fascinating history of Sweden during the Cold War. Let's discover some facts about Swedish politics, society, economy, culture, and foreign policy.

341. **The Cold War was a period in the 20th century when there were tensions between communist and capitalist ideologies.** The United States and its allies represented the West and capitalism, and the Soviet Union and its allies embraced communism.

342. **Sweden stayed neutral as part of its policy of neutrality,** which meant it wouldn't take sides or ally with either side during an armed conflict.

343. **Sweden's strategic location and neutral status made it a prime target for espionage by both the Soviet Union and the West during the Cold War.** The country's intelligence agencies also played a role in gathering intelligence on both sides. **While Sweden was not directly involved in the conflict,** its territory was used as a staging ground for spies and their operations.

344. **Sweden continued trading with both sides since it didn't take a political stance.** For example, it was able to export goods from both Western Europe and Eastern Europe.

345. **Sweden sought ways to reduce global tensions through diplomacy. In the 1970s, it hosted the Stockholm Conference** for East and West German politicians to discuss improving relations between their countries.

346. One of **the things the Stockholm Conference accomplished was setting up a direct line of communication between the US and USSR** to help avoid a misunderstanding that might lead to nuclear war.

347. **Though a small number of people in Sweden advocated joining NATO against an aggressive Soviet Union, most Swedes enthusiastically supported neutrality.**

348. Sweden's economy grew during this time. Sweden was one of the richest nations in the world during the Cold War.

349. During this period, **Sweden was noted for its zealous guarding of its air and seas.** There were many instances when airplanes and vessels (mostly from the Soviet Union) were warned to stay out of the area and escorted out by Swedish forces.

350. In 1985, **Swedish Prime Minister Olof Palme was assassinated while walking home after watching a movie with his family.** This shocked the world and caused much grief in Sweden, as Palme was seen as a symbol of peace and hope for many people.

351. No one was ever arrested for Palme's murder. One popular theory is that since Palme was a strong advocate for peace and disarmament, a foreign intelligence agency might have killed him in order to silence him.

352. Sweden used its neutrality to help facilitate negotiations between the East and West toward the end of The Cold War. The nation helped bring about an agreement on nuclear arms reductions between US President Ronald Reagan and Soviet General Secretary Mikhail Gorbachev in 1988 (known as the Reykjavik Summit).

353. Despite not being part of any political alliances or blocs during this time, Sweden remained engaged in international politics. Sweden sent troops abroad on UN Peacekeeping missions, such as those in Lebanon, Cambodia, and Kuwait, throughout the Cold War era.

354. During the 1980s, **Sweden opened its doors** to over **100,000 refugees** from Chile and Vietnam, which were affected by political unrest.

355. In 1991, **Sweden became one of the first countries to recognize Estonia's independence from the Soviet Union.** The Soviet Union would collapse later that year.

356. With global tensions easing after years of conflict, **Sweden was able to focus on other issues, such as environmental protection and climate change.** It even ratified a treaty aiming to reduce atmospheric pollution (the Kyoto Protocol).

357. **Sweden has been considered one of the most progressive countries in Europe since before WWII,** but it made great strides forward during the Cold War. It has pioneered social reforms such as same-sex marriage and equal access to education and healthcare regardless of income or background.

358. **The country continues to play a significant role in international diplomacy through organizations such as the UN Security Council,** where Swedish representatives often act as mediators between different parties involved in disputes.

359. **Since the Cold War period, Sweden has become an increasingly diverse society,** with people from all over the world coming to settle there and contributing notably toward its culture and economy.

360. In 2022, **Sweden asked to join NATO as a result of the Russian invasion of Ukraine. If it joins NATO,** that means its two-hundred-year-old policy of neutrality would be officially over.

The Feminist and Equal Rights Movement
(1970s–1990s)

This chapter will explore major social movements in Sweden, such as **the feminist movement.** Examine **how these movements impacted Swedish society, politics, and culture.**

361. **The feminist movement in Sweden began around the 1970s** and was a big part of Swedish society during the 1980s and 1990s.

362. **Two of the key events of the early part of this era were the publication of the book Kvinnofrigörelsen och vi** (The Women's Liberation Movement and Us) in 1969 and the founding of **the Feministiskt Forum** (Feminist Forum) in 1972, bringing women from all over Sweden together in Stockholm.

363. **The feminist movement aimed to create equality between men and women in all areas,** such as legal rights, voting rights, access to education, job opportunities, and political representation.

364. **Its supporters argued for greater parity between genders in terms of pay at work,** equal parental leave policies, increased opportunities for female representation in politics, and improved childcare services so that mothers could return to their careers after childbirth or raising young children.

365. **Swedish feminists fought hard for equal rights within marriage,** such as shared responsibility over children's upbringing and joint legal custody if the couple separated or divorced; these reforms were achieved by 1988.

366. Before 1988, **Swedish law gave the father automatic custody of children in the event of a divorce.** This meant the mother had to fight for custody, and she often lost. The feminist movement argued this was unfair and discriminatory, and they demanded that the law be changed.

367. In 1995, **Sweden amended its abortion law so that it could be carried out without a doctor's approval,** thus ensuring greater autonomy for women.

368. **The Feminist Initiative** (FI) **Party was formed in 2005** to create a gender-equal society through political representation. Its popularity has waxed and waned. Though it was once a majority party in some small towns, it has lost much of its following.

369. **During this period, women in Sweden had higher employment rates than many other countries.** By 1990, almost half of all Swedish civil servants were female.

370. **Women began entering traditionally male-dominated fields,** such as engineering, medicine, and business management, during this period.

371. In 1994, **the Equality Act came into force, which prohibited discrimination on any grounds related to sex, ethnicity, or disability,** further enshrining protections for marginalized groups within society despite resistance from some conservative politicians at that time.

372. In the mid-1990s, **Sweden became one of the first countries to introduce a law that allowed same-sex couples to have legally recognized unions.**

373. In 2009, **same-sex marriage was made legal.** This legislation earned international attention for its progressive stance on **LGBTQ+ rights.**

374. **Swedish feminists were also active in promoting greater access to sexual education in schools,** as well as improved services related to reproductive health care, such as contraception advice or abortion services.

375. **In 1996, laws around parental leave changed so that both parents had equal rights when it came to taking time off work after having a baby.** Before then, fathers could only take 14 days, while mothers were entitled to up to 180 days with 80 percent pay rate. Today, they can share up to 490 days between them at an adjusted salary depending on how much each has taken overall.

376. Swedish women's organizations lobbied for increased support for victims of domestic violence and sexual assault, greater rights and protection for sex workers, and the introduction of gender quotas in politics to ensure more female representation within government.

377. The feminist movement contributed toward a change in attitudes about motherhood. In the early 19th century, raising children was seen almost entirely as a woman's responsibility, but feminists argued that men should have an equal role, which resulted in increased paternity leave provisions.

378. Sweden is striving for equal pay for equal work. The Discrimination Act of 2009 states that employers and employees should work actively to even out the pay gap between the sexes.

379. However, a significant pay gap remains, which is one of the challenges on the Swedish gender equality agenda. In 2022, a woman's average monthly salary in Sweden was 90.1 percent of the average man's.

380. In 2015, **women made up 45 percent of Parliament, 45 percent of local legislatures, and 52 percent of national government ministers.**

Abortion Law Reform
(1974–1976)

This chapter will explore the process of abortion law reform in Sweden. Look at how this period saw significant changes to **Swedish laws surrounding access to abortions and its impact on public health.** Additionally, we'll discuss the different arguments for and against the reform, as well as examine whether or not it achieved its desired outcomes. Finally, we'll consider how other countries have used similar methods when reforming their laws regarding abortion rights.

381. In the 1930s, **abortion was only permitted in Sweden under certain tragic circumstances,** like rape, incest, and the health of the mother. This was still more progressive than most other Western countries at the time.

382. In 1975, **the Swedish Parliament passed a law that allowed abortion** within the first eighteen weeks of pregnancy with no questions asked.

383. **The law made it easier for women to get abortions in Sweden** and helped reduce maternal mortality rates due to unsafe abortions.

384. **However, there were some restrictions based on age and other criteria such as mental illness.**

385. **This change drastically reduced illegal abortions happening outside official medical facilities.** Illegal abortions are often dangerous for the mother. At the time, there was no legal protection if something went wrong during the procedure.

Economic Crisis of the 1980s

This chapter will explore the economic crisis of the 1980s and its effects on Sweden. Examine facts about this period, including **how the crisis impacted Swedish society,** its economy, and politics.

386. **The economic crisis of the 1980s hit Sweden hard,** causing a deep recession and forcing many in the country to rethink many of its economic and expensive social policies.

387. **The crisis led to a debate about the future of Sweden's social welfare system.** Some people argued the system was too expensive and needed to be reformed. Others argued the system was essential to the Swedish way of life and should be protected.

388. **Unemployment jumped from around 2 percent to 8 percent,** as businesses and industries struggled with high interest rates and low investment levels. The peak unemployment rate was 10.2 percent, which was reached in 1993.

389. **The Swedish government implemented cuts in public spending and increased taxes to try and reduce budget deficits.** These austerity measures were unpopular with many people, but they were seen as necessary to stabilize the economy.

390. **The measures were successful in reducing the budget deficit, but they also had a negative impact on the economy.** The cuts in public spending led to a decline in social welfare benefits and a reduction in public services. The increase in taxes made it more difficult for businesses to invest and create jobs.

391. By 1985, **inflation had become so severe that consumer prices were rising faster than wages,** which caused a decrease in living standards for people regardless of their income level or social class.

392. **The inflation rate in Sweden reached a peak of 15.5 percent in 1980.** This meant the prices of goods and services were rising by 13.6 percent each year.

393. **To help tackle these issues, the government introduced new economic policies, such as wage-earner funds,** where tax money could be invested directly into businesses instead of the state.

394. **Because of wage-earner funds, businesses could access capital easily, and Sweden's economy recovered faster than other European countries.** However, some economists argue that wage-earner funds were too small to make a real difference in the economy and that the economic recovery was due to other factors, such as the government's austerity measures.

395. **Despite the economic crisis, the Swedish industry remained relatively strong due to its focus on innovation and technology,** which enabled it to be competitive with international companies.

396. **The government introduced policies such as the deregulation, privatization, and liberalization of markets,** which further aided the recovery process by allowing increased competition between firms operating within a market.

397. **Though a number of steps had been taken to ease the economic crisis in Sweden by the end of the 1980s,** some effects, like high unemployment rates, lingered into the early 1990s.

398. **Sweden managed to reduce its national debt from 80 percent of GDP** (gross domestic product) in 1983 to just 37 percent by 2016—an impressive feat considering how deep its economic crisis was during that period.

399. **The Swedish government sold a number of state-owned assets,** which helped to raise revenue and reduce the government's debt. These included the state-owned monopoly on alcohol production and the famous Saab Corporation.

400. **The Swedish banking system has been strengthened since the economic crisis,** with all major banks now required to hold at least 12 percent capital reserves compared to 2 to 4 percent before this crisis happened. This means that Swedish banks are in a much stronger financial position than they were in the 1980s.

Sweden's European Union Membership
(1995)

This chapter will explore Sweden's journey to becoming a member of the European Union. Look at notable events that led to this, including negotiations and referendums, and discover how Sweden changed after joining this political union.

401. **As an EU member, Sweden has access to the world's largest single market,** with five hundred million consumers and businesses that buy and sell goods within it without paying tariffs on imports or exports.

402. **There are some challenges associated with being an EU member.** For example, Sweden has to comply with EU regulations, which can be costly and time-consuming. However, the benefits of membership outweigh the challenges.

403. **Since joining the EU, trade with other EU members has increased significantly for Swedish companies,** which means more job opportunities for Swedes.

404. **Swedes can move and live in any other country within the EU as long as they respect local laws.** They also enjoy shared rights like healthcare coverage if living abroad temporarily for work purposes.

405. **Being part of the European Union helps protect Swedish citizens from crime by working together on issues like terrorism prevention.**

406. **Sweden has become increasingly influential in making decisions for the EU,** including contributing to its climate change targets and joining peacekeeping operations.

407. **Swedes benefit from cheaper goods and services thanks to the competition law,** which keeps prices low across all EU markets.

408. **Sweden's membership has allowed the nation to participate in decisions regarding trade agreements with other countries outside of the European Union,** such as Japan and China, so it can take advantage of new opportunities offered by those countries.

409. **The Swedish government contributes money annually toward projects that help people living inside and outside the European Union have better lives.** This includes helping refugees find safety within their borders.

410. **Sweden, unlike many EU countries, has not adopted the euro, the currency of the European Union.** The Swedish kroner is the currency in Sweden today.

Integration Program, Immigration, and Asylum Seekers
(1990s–2000s)

This chapter will explore the integration program in Sweden. Analyze how policies developed during this period impacted immigrants and asylum seekers, and discover some of the challenges faced by both migrants and policymakers when it came to long-term settlement within this Nordic country.

411. **The Swedish government implemented an integration program to help newcomers settle in Sweden faster and easier.**

412. **This program focused on helping people learn Swedish, find jobs,** get healthcare coverage, and access housing services if needed.

413. It also provided information **about how to adapt to living in Sweden** more successfully by teaching them about its culture, laws, and customs.

414. **A significant part of this integration plan was for asylum seekers** who had fled their home countries due to war or political unrest. They were offered special protection under international law, which allowed them a safe space to start a new life free of fear.

415. **The number of asylum seekers increased dramatically during the 1990s when refugees started arriving from Kosovo. Refugees came from Afghanistan** soon afterward when US troops invaded in 2001.

416. **The Aliens Act enabled anyone who had lived in Sweden for five years or more to apply for permanent residency,** which helped many newcomers gain official status within their new home country much sooner than before.

417. **Education is an integral part of integration since it gives immigrants better opportunities when trying to find employment,** so special language classes became available at schools that focused on teaching Swedish and other subjects like math and science.

418. **The Swedish government created welcome centers around 2002,** which provided detailed information about living in Sweden, including how taxes work and where healthcare facilities could be found. These centers are still operational today and offer support to all immigrants regardless of their background.

419. **The government provided financial assistance for refugees who needed it and subsidized housing in some areas,** which helped everyone have access to necessities while they adjusted to life in Sweden.

420. **There are dedicated organizations working toward helping asylum seekers integrate into Swedish society,** such as the Association of Newcomers (Nyföreningsrådet), which offers legal advice and language courses at discounted prices, or Red Cross refugee camps, where people can find temporary accommodations until they get settled somewhere more permanent.

421. **The number of immigrants has increased over the years, with people coming from all over the world,** such as Syria, Afghanistan, and Iraq. Sweden has a very generous policy when it comes to accepting refugees seeking safety within its borders.

422. **An integral part of integration is understanding how Social Security works so that immigrants can get the support they need if something unexpected were to happen.** Sweden has created online tutorials available that explain everything from healthcare benefits to employment rights in an easy-to-understand way.

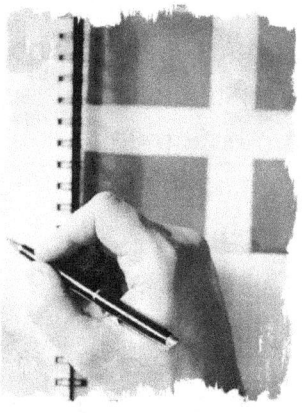

423. **One of the biggest challenges faced by asylum seekers in Sweden has been finding a job,** as employers often have reservations about hiring someone who doesn't speak fluent Swedish or isn't familiar with local customs. **Many initiatives, such as vocational training and language classes, have been implemented,** which help make it easier for newcomers to gain meaningful employment.

424. **After the flood of refugees from the Middle East arrived in northern Europe,** there was a backlash. As a result, many of the laws passed in the years immediately after 2001 have been rescinded or become more restrictive.

425. **Today, residence permits are harder to get and must be approved every five years. Citizenship depends on Swedish language knowledge and having a job,** and border controls have been tightened.

Anti-Racist Popular Resistance Movement
(2000s)

Let's discover some interesting facts about **why this movement arose, its goals and tactics,** and how they tackled major Swedish political issues.

426. **This movement began as a reaction to violence toward immigrants and non-Nordic Swedish citizens.**

427. **There were anti-immigration riots in the southern city of Malmo in the 1980s in which some extreme right-wing movements were involved.** This was partially responsible for the rise of the anti-racism movement in Sweden. Since 2015, there have been disturbances in more cities.

428. **The movement uses protests, marches, rallies, demonstrations, petitions,** and other forms of activism to achieve justice and equality. The movement has organized several events throughout Sweden, with hundreds, if not thousands, attending them.

429. **The movement's main goal is to end discrimination based on race or ethnicity in Swedish society by fighting against all forms of racism,** including institutionalized racism from governmental institutions like police departments or courts of law.

430. **Members of the movement provide education through workshops about structural oppression-related topics,** such as understanding white privilege and recognizing microaggressions and how they can affect people differently.

431. **In recent years, it has also started the #MyFreedomDay campaign** to encourage people to recognize and fight human trafficking.

432. In 2018, **Sweden's Parliament passed an anti-discrimination law that prohibits discrimination** based on race or ethnicity, which was one of the main goals of this movement.

433. **The popular movement against racism has been a significant factor in bringing awareness to racial issues in Sweden,** such as **Black Lives Matter protests** and other solidarity initiatives with communities facing similar struggles all over Europe and beyond.

434. **The movement emphasizes creating safe spaces for minorities** so they can share their experiences without fear while still demanding change from institutions responsible for oppression and injustice.

435. **It also works closely with other organizations fighting for social justice,** like Amnesty International and Human Rights Watch.

Same-sex Marriage Legislation
(2009)

This chapter will explore **the legalization of same-sex marriage in Sweden**, focusing on how it came to be accepted and passed into Swedish law. We'll also look at the impact this legislation has had on **LGBT couples living in Sweden.**

436. In 2009, **Sweden legalized same-sex marriage. Prior to that,** Sweden had recognized registered partnerships for same-sex couples, which provided some legal rights and protections.

437. **The Church of Sweden began performing weddings for same-sex couples in 2009**

438. In 2015, **it was estimated that around four thousand marriages between people of the same gender occurred in Sweden in just five years.**

439. Since 2013, **any person who has lived outside of Sweden for more than two years can get legally married there even if they are not from European Union countries** or hold a residence permit.

440. As of October 2023, **Sweden was one of only thirty-four countries worldwide that allowed same-sex marriages.**

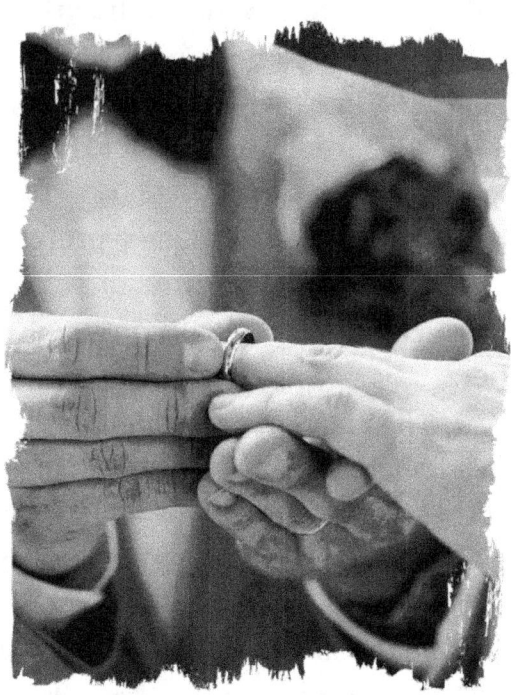

Sustainable Development and Environmental Policies (2010s)

This chapter **will explore sustainability strategies and environmental policies in Sweden.** Look at how groundbreaking sustainable development initiatives implemented by **Swedish authorities have led to energy efficiency and renewable energy sources.** Additionally, examine some notable challenges facing Sweden's environmental policymakers today.

441. As of 2021, **Sweden's renewable energy sources, such as wind and hydropower,** provide more than half of the country's electricity needs.

442. **Sweden has set a goal to become climate neutral by 2045,** which means producing zero emissions.

443. **The government banned some disposable plastics like bags and straws in 2021 to reduce pollution levels in nature reserves, forests, oceans, and rivers.** The ban also includes polystyrene (Styrofoam) containers, balloons, and wet wipes.

444. **Sweden is one of the leading countries in the world in terms of recycling and waste reduction. In 2020,** Sweden recycled nearly 99 percent of its plastic bottles and 95 percent of its paper and cardboard.

445. To combat air pollution from motor vehicles, **electric-only zones have been created in major urban areas across the country,** resulting in cleaner air quality.

446. **There is an increasing trend toward using digital technology solutions like online meetings,** which reduce traveling time and costs and help lower emissions.

447. **Sweden has set aside 9 percent of its total land area for nature conservation,** which helps protect biodiversity and endangered species from harm.

448. **Several green initiatives have been taken in the agricultural sector,** like using fewer chemicals, better crop rotation systems, and organic production methods, which help improve sustainability while preserving soil fertility and water quality.

449. **To encourage people to save energy at home and work,** there are tax deductions available when purchasing items that use less electricity or gas, **such as LED bulbs or energy-efficient appliances.**

450. **Sweden has pledged its commitment toward global climate action.** It has signed up to the Paris Agreement with other nations and made firm promises about reducing CO_2 levels by 2030.

PROTECT

"Open-door" Refugee Policy
(2015–2016)

This chapter will discuss Sweden's open-door refugee policy. We'll explore how it impacted Swedish society, its political sphere, and its economic landscape. You will also gain insight into why this decision was taken.

451. **Though Sweden has treated refugees well since the end of WWII, it has never been an "open country,"** which means it does not allow just anyone to come into the country. There have been quotas on the number of arrivals. However, it has been recognized that **Sweden is one of the most progressive countries** when it comes to taking in refugees from troubled parts of the world.

452. **Refugees from countries like Syria, Iraq, and Afghanistan** were able to seek asylum in Sweden in the early 2000s.

453. In 2015, a flood of refugees from **the Middle East came to western Europe and Scandinavia,** fleeing war, repression, and poverty. This happened so quickly that it took many countries by surprise. Many political and social complications arose.

454. **During 2015 and 2016, nearly 200,000 applications for asylum were submitted by individuals seeking refuge in Sweden** alone—the highest ever recorded number of refugee applications since World War II.

455. **The open-door policy was controversial throughout Europe because it meant a large influx of people entering the region all at once.** However, many Swedes supported this decision with donations and volunteer efforts to aid those who needed help.

456. **To help integrate refugees into society, the Swedish government** offered language classes and job-training programs.

457. **The open-door policy had an economic impact on Sweden's GDP,** as money spent on supporting refugee populations rose. It helped stimulate the economy during a time of need.

458. **The Swedish government's open-door policy was limited in 2016 due to increasing pressure from Swedish citizens,** conservative political parties, and other European countries that were being flooded with refugees.

459. **The Swedish government has worked to increase cooperation with other European nations** to ensure that refugees are not sent back to their countries of origin without first receiving the proper legal documentation and protection from possible persecution. This has had varying levels of success.

460. To this day, **Sweden continues to provide support for those seeking refuge by offering language courses, job opportunities, and access to healthcare services,** such as mental health resources.

Swedish Government Today
(2020–2023)

This chapter **will explore the current state of the Swedish government and its unique and fascinating political system.** We'll also **discover how this small Nordic nation has managed to remain one of the most stable democracies in Europe** despite being home to diverse cultures, languages, religions, and ideologies.

461. **Sweden has a parliamentary democracy**, which means that the people elect representatives to form the government.

462. **The prime minister is the leader of the government** and is appointed by **the Riksdag** (Swedish Parliament).

463. **Sweden is divided into twenty-one counties,** each with a county council responsible for local issues like health care and schools.

464. **National laws in Sweden are made by Parliament** (the Riksdag). Representatives from all over Sweden come together to discuss important matters affecting everyone in the country.

465. **The king and queen of Sweden have a notable but symbolic role as head of state.** They don't have political power, which makes them similar to the monarch of the United Kingdom.

466. **Sweden's Constitution guarantees freedom of speech and equal rights for all citizens regardless of sex, religion, and ethnicity.**

467. **To become a law, proposed laws must pass through three "readings" for approval at different levels before being voted on by members elected to Parliament.** The first reading is a general debate in the Riksdag. The second reading is a more detailed debate, and the third reading is a vote on whether to pass the law.

468. **Income tax in Sweden is based on a progressive system,** where higher earners pay more than those with lower incomes.

469. **Sweden has been ranked one of the most gender-equal countries in the world** thanks to government policy initiatives that have promoted gender equality.

470. **The official language spoken by all Swedes is Swedish,** but English is widely taught from an early age. A number of Swedes of Finnish descent, especially in the east, also speak Finnish.

471. **Sweden has conscription (military draft). However,** it is a "partial conscription," meaning that only a small percentage of eligible people are conscripted. The length of required service is about one year, which is much shorter than it used to be.

472. **The Riksdag consists of 349 seats representing various political parties across the country.** These parties are divided into eight different blocs that represent opposing political views.

473. **The indigenous Sámi people of Sweden have their own political body called Sametinget. Sametinget was established in 1993** and currently has thirty-one members who are elected by the Sámi people. **The Sametinget addresses issues unique to the Sámi people,** especially land rights, discrimination, and language education.

474. **Sweden has one of the highest tax rates among EU countries,** as well as high-quality public services, including health care, education, and social benefits.

475. **The Swedish government works with several international organizations like UNICEF, WHO** (World Health Organization), and **UNESCO** to help people have access to basic human rights.

Swedish Celebrities
(1970–Present)

From the last part of the 20th century to today, there have been many **world-famous Swedish celebrities,** from singers to tennis players. Here is a list of some of the most recognized Swedes from 1970 to today.

476. The Swedish pop group ABBA, formed in 1972, consisted of four members: **Agnetha Fältskog, Björn Ulvaeus, Benny Andersson,** and **Anni-Frid Lyngstad.** They achieved international fame with their catchy hits and became one of the best-selling music acts of all time.

477. Björn Borg is a legendary tennis player who won eleven Grand Slam singles titles in his career, including **six French Open and five Wimbledon championships.** He is known for his cool demeanor on the court and his iconic headbands.

478. Greta Thunberg, born in 2003, gained **worldwide recognition for her climate activism.** She started the Fridays for Future school strike movement, inspiring millions of young people to demand action on climate change.

479. Alexander Skarsgård is a Swedish actor known for his roles in True Blood, Big Little Lies, and Tarzan. He comes from a family of actors, including his father, **Stellan Skarsgård,** and his brothers, **Gustaf, Bill,** and **Valter.**

480. Alicia Vikander is an Academy Award-winning actress who gained fame for her role in the film **The Danish Girl.** She also appeared in **Ex Machina, Tomb Raider, and The Man from U.N.C.L.E.**

481. Zlatan Ibrahimović is a Swedish citizen of Bosnian-Croatian descent who is a professional footballer renowned for his exceptional skills and goal-scoring abilities. He has played for some of the top football clubs in the world, including FC Barcelona, Paris Saint-Germain, and Manchester United.

482. Robyn is a prominent Swedish singer and songwriter known for her unique style and hits like **"Dancing on My Own," "Call Your Girlfriend," and "With Every Heartbeat."** She has been influential in the electronic and pop music scenes.

483. The late Max von Sydow was a Swedish actor who appeared in numerous acclaimed films, including Ingmar Bergman's classics The Seventh Seal and Wild Strawberries. He had a successful international career spanning several decades.

484. Noomi Rapace is a Swedish actress who gained international recognition for her role as Lisbeth Salander in the original Swedish film adaptations of Stieg Larsson's Millennium series. She has also appeared in Hollywood productions like **Prometheus and Sherlock Holmes: A Game of Shadows.**

485. Tim Bergling, known professionally as Avicii, was a highly influential Swedish DJ, producer, and songwriter. He achieved worldwide success with hits like **"Levels," "Wake Me Up," and "Hey Brother"** before his untimely death in 2018.

The Sámi People of Sweden
(10,000 BCE–Present)

The Sámi are an indigenous people who have inhabited Sápmi, a region in northern Europe that encompasses parts of Sweden, Norway, Finland, and Russia, for thousands of years. They have traditionally practiced a **semi-nomadic lifestyle,** herding reindeer and fishing for their livelihood. The Sámi also have a strong oral tradition, and their mythology and folktales are passed down from generation to generation. In recent centuries, **the Sámi have faced many challenges,** including assimilation policies by the governments of the countries in which they live.
Let's take a look at how the Sámi have evolved throughout the centuries.

486. **The first known Sámi settlements in Sweden appeared in 10,000 BCE.**

487. **The earliest known written mention of the Sámi people was by the Roman historian Tacitus** in his collection of writings called Germania, published in the 1st century CE. **He described them as nomadic people** who lived in the northernmost parts of Europe and practiced hunting and fishing.

488. **The Sámi are believed to have originated in northern Europe, but their exact origins are still unknown.** Some scholars believe that they are descended from **the Paleo-Siberian** peoples who migrated to the region from Asia thousands of years ago. Others believe they are more closely related to the Finno-Ugric peoples, who are native to northern Europe.

489. **After Swedish independence from Denmark, Sweden claimed all Sámi lands within its borders.**

490. In the 1600s, **the Swedish government began to implement policies aimed at assimilating the Sámi people,** including forced conversion to Christianity and the prohibition of the Sámi language.

491. In the 1800s, **the Swedish government established boarding schools for Sámi children,** where they were forbidden to speak their own language or practice their traditional culture. This continued into the 1970s.

492. **These schools were located in remote areas of Sweden, and Sámi children were forced to attend them,** even if it meant being separated from their families for long periods of time.

493. **According to the Sámi Parliament of Sweden, Sámi people were sterilized under the Swedish government's racial hygiene policy,** which was in place from the 1930s to the 1970s. The policy was based on the belief that certain groups of people were genetically inferior and should be prevented from reproducing.

494. In the 1970s, **Sweden began to relax its assimilation policies toward the Sámi,** but much of Sámi culture and history had already been lost.

495. **The industrialization of Sweden and the loss of reindeer habitat** led many Sámi to take jobs in parts of Sweden far from their traditional lands in the north of the country.

496. **In 1917, the first Sámi congress was held, calling for greater autonomy for the Sámi people.**

497. In the 1950s, **the Sámi Cultural Council was established** to promote the Sámi culture and language.

498. In 1993, **the Sámi Parliament of Sweden was established,** giving the Sámi people a voice in their own affairs. **The Sámi seek to promote education in the Sámi languages,** protect the rights of reindeer herders, have a voice in how decisions are made regarding natural resources and environmental protection, **and negotiate with the Swedish government** on questions about healthcare, social services, and housing.

499. As of October 2023, **Sweden has not ratified the ILO Convention on Indigenous and Tribal Peoples,** which would recognize the rights of the Sámi people.

500. **There are ten Sámi languages spoken in Sweden, Finland, Norway, and Russia.** The Sámi languages are all endangered, and efforts are under way to preserve them.

Conclusion

The story of Sweden has been one of remarkable progress and change. From prehistoric times to the present, the country has gone through a great deal to become the nation it is today.

The Viking Age expanded Swedish territory and brought warring clans together under a unifying banner. The Kalmar Union solidified this unity, while Danish rule introduced new forms of governance. In more recent times, **Swedish politics has seen many reforms,** particularly those aimed at gender equality, immigrants, and climate change.

While this book has provided an overview of the history of Sweden, it is only a primer to further **explore this nation's rich past.** It takes more than just reading one book to understand how nations have gotten to where they are today. **We encourage you to check out our sources and read more about the fascinating history of Sweden!**

If you enjoyed this book, a review on Amazon would be greatly appreciated because it would mean a lot to hear from you.

To leave a review:

1. Open your camera app.
2. Point your mobile device at the QR code.
3. The review page will appear in your web browser.

Thanks for your support!

Check out another book in the series

Welcome Aboard, Check Out This Limited-Time Free Bonus!

Ahoy, reader! Welcome to the Ahoy Publications family, and thanks for snagging a copy of this book! Since you've chosen to join us on this journey, we'd like to offer you something special.

Check out the link below for a FREE e-book filled with delightful facts about American History.

But that's not all - you'll also have access to our exclusive email list with even more free e-books and insider knowledge. Well, what are ye waiting for? Click the link below to join and set sail toward exciting adventures in American History.

Access your bonus here: https://ahoypublications.com/

Or, Scan the QR code!

Sources and Additional References

"Prehistoric Sweden," VisitSweden, https://www.visitsweden.com/sweden-culture/prehistoric-sweden/.

"History of Sweden: Prehistory and Antiquity — Ancient Scandinavia Encyclopedia," Ancient History Encyclopedia, October 10 2016, www.ancient.eu/scandinavia_prehistory_antiquity/.

Price, Neil S., ed. (2002). The Viking Way: Religion and War in Late Iron Age Scandinavia. Uppsala University Press.

Gregory, Marcus Jeffrey. Medieval Scandinavia: An Encyclopedia (Routledge Encyclopedias of the Middle Ages). Taylor and Francis Group, 2017.

"Viking Age." Sweden History Museum, www.swedenhistorymuseum.se/en/the-viking-age/.

Högberg, Jan-Olov et al., eds. A History of the Nordic Countries. Brill, 2017.

"Medieval Swedish Literature | History and Facts." Britannica, Encyclopedia Britannica, Inc., www.britannica.com/topic/medieval-Swedish-literature.

Stokstad, Marilyn. "Medieval Sweden: History and Culture". Encyclopedia Britannica, 13 Nov 2018, https://www.britannica.com/place/Sweden/Medieval-Sweden.

Gottfried, Robert S., et al., eds. "Kalmar Union (1397–1523)." Encyclopedia Britannica https://www.britannica.com/event/Kalmar-Union-1397-1523.

"Christopher III of Denmark." Encyclopedia Britannica, https://www.britannica.com/biography/Christopher-III-king-of-Denmark.

"History of Sweden." Accessed June 4, 2020. https://www.britannica.com/place/Sweden/History-of-Sweden#ref1136145.

Hartley Larkin C. The Life of Gustavus Adolphus. Charles Scribner's Sons Publishers Company New York NY USA, 1868.

Smith, Jonathan R. Sweden in World War II and After (1939–2017). ABC-CLIO, 2019.

"The Great Northern War (1700-1721)." Encyclopedia Britannica, Encyclopedia Britannica, Inc., 25 Aug. 2020, https://www.britannica.com/event/Great-Northern-War#ref528866/.

Albin Widén and Lars Trägårdh, The History of Sweden (London: Routledge, 2013).

Ann-Marie Ekengren et al., eds., A History of Modern Sweden (New York: Palgrave Macmillan, 2011).

Olof Ruin, Political Parties and Party Systems in the Nordic Countries (Stockholm: Almqvist and Wiksell International, 1993).

Lindqvist, Sven Erik. A Short History of Sweden: From Prehistory to the Present Day. Routledge Press, 2015.